AMAZING ART FORMS

The Art of Theater

BY K. A. HALE

Kids Core

An Imprint of Abdo Publishing
abdobooks.com

abdobooks.com

Published by Abdo Publishing, a division of ABDO, PO Box 398166, Minneapolis, Minnesota 55439.

Printed in the United States of America, North Mankato, Minnesota.
102024
012025

THIS BOOK CONTAINS RECYCLED MATERIALS

Cover Photos: Shutterstock Images (masks); Fer Gregory/Shutterstock Images (background)
Interior Photos: Shutterstock Images, 4–5, 14, 15, 18, 28 (top), 29 (top); Yuganov Konstantin/Shutterstock Images, 7; Hulton Archive/Getty Images, 8; Monkey Business Images/Shutterstock Images, 10–11; Narcis Parfenti/Shutterstock Images, 12 (top left); John Kane/Flickr, 12 (top right); Katharine Hale/Red Line Editorial, 12 (bottom left); Andrius Zemaitis/Shutterstock Images, 12 (bottom right); Noam Galai/Getty Images for Cats/Getty Images Entertainment/Getty Images, 17; Noam Galai/Getty Images Entertainment/Getty Images, 20–21; Oli Scarff/Getty Images News/Getty Images, 23; Theo Wargo/Getty Images for Tony Awards Productions/Getty Images Entertainment/Getty Images, 24; Dia Dipasupil/Getty Images Entertainment/Getty Images, 25; SOPA Images Limited/Alamy Live News/Alamy, 26; Wavebreak Media/Shutterstock Images, 28 (bottom); Jim Polakis/Shutterstock Images, 29 (bottom)

Editor: Haley Williams
Series Designer: Katharine Hale

Library of Congress Control Number: 2024938396

Publisher's Cataloging-in-Publication Data

Names: Hale, K. A., author.
Title: The art of theater / by K. A. Hale
Description: Minneapolis, Minnesota: ABDO Publishing, 2025 | Series: Amazing art forms | Includes online resources and index.
Identifiers: ISBN 9781098295820 (lib. bdg.) | ISBN 9798384916826 (ebook)
Subjects: LCSH: Art--Juvenile literature. | Theater--Juvenile literature. | Art and theater--Juvenile literature. | Stage actors--Juvenile literature. | Theater and society--Juvenile literature. | Arts and history--Juvenile literature.
Classification: DDC 792--dc23

CONTENTS

CHAPTER 1
Opening Night 4

CHAPTER 2
Creating Theater 10

CHAPTER 3
People and Places in Theater 20

Art Supplies 28
Glossary 30
Online Resources 31
Learn More 31
Index 32
About the Author 32

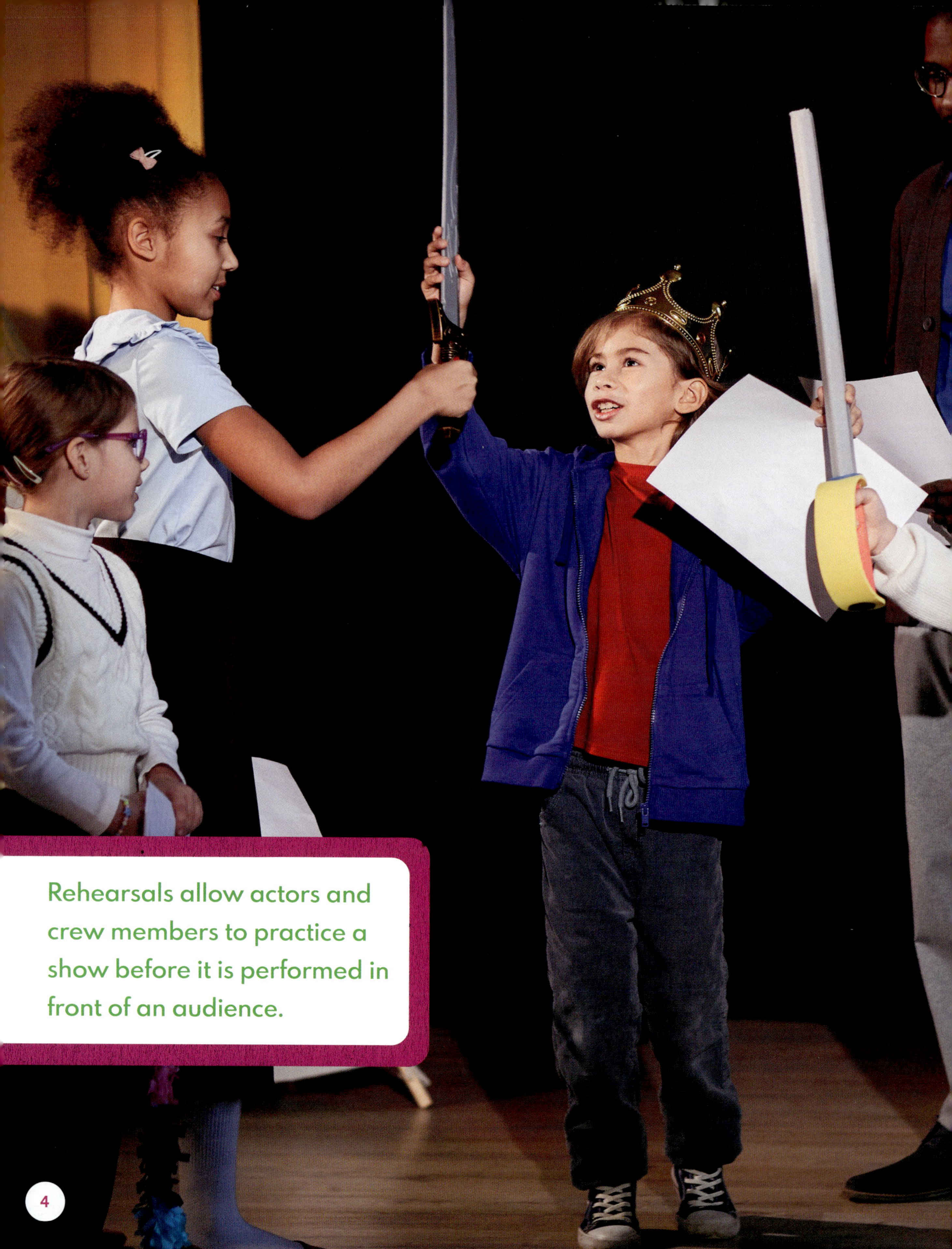

Rehearsals allow actors and crew members to practice a show before it is performed in front of an audience.

CHAPTER 1

Opening Night

"I am the very model of a modern major general," Aiden says with his castmates. The kids all say the tongue twister faster and faster, adding silly hand motions. They are using it as a warm-up before performing in their school musical.

Actors use warm-ups like stretches. They get their bodies, mouths, and voices ready to perform. The music director leads Aiden and his castmates through different singing exercises. Once they are done, it is time to finish getting ready to go on stage.

Aiden goes to the dressing room. He puts on his costume and makeup. He also rehearses

Ancient Greek Theater

Theater has a history that is thousands of years old. Ancient Greeks performed plays called comedies and tragedies. A **chorus** would sing and dance. Actors would play many roles. They used masks to represent their characters' emotions. Plays were performed in large, outdoor theaters. Some of these ancient plays, such as *Oedipus Rex*, are still performed today.

Dressing rooms often have mirrors with bright lights to help performers see while putting on their makeup and costumes.

his lines in his head. It is opening night, and Aiden is a little nervous. But he is also excited. The cast has been working on the show for months. Aiden's whole family has come to watch him perform.

A crew member says, "Places, everyone!" Aiden goes to the stage. He takes a deep breath to calm his nerves. Then the curtain goes up and the stage lights turn on. The orchestra plays, and Aiden begins singing and dancing.

Theater productions became a popular form of entertainment in the United States during the 1800s and 1900s.

At the end of the show, the crowd cheers. The cast takes a bow. Aiden smiles. He cannot wait to do it all again tomorrow!

All the World's a Stage

Theater is the art of performing for an audience. It is a kind of storytelling. There are many types of theater. Operas tell stories through music. Ballets tell stories through dance. In plays and musicals, actors use words, songs, and their bodies to tell stories.

There are several ways to get involved in theater. Many schools have theater departments. Some people do theater as a job. Others do it for fun. People can perform on stage, help behind the scenes, or enjoy shows from the audience. Theater has something to offer everyone.

Further Evidence

Look at the website below. Does it give any new evidence to support Chapter One?

What Is Theater?

abdocorelibrary.com/art-of-theater

During improvised theater performances, actors sometimes ask for scene and character suggestions from the audience.

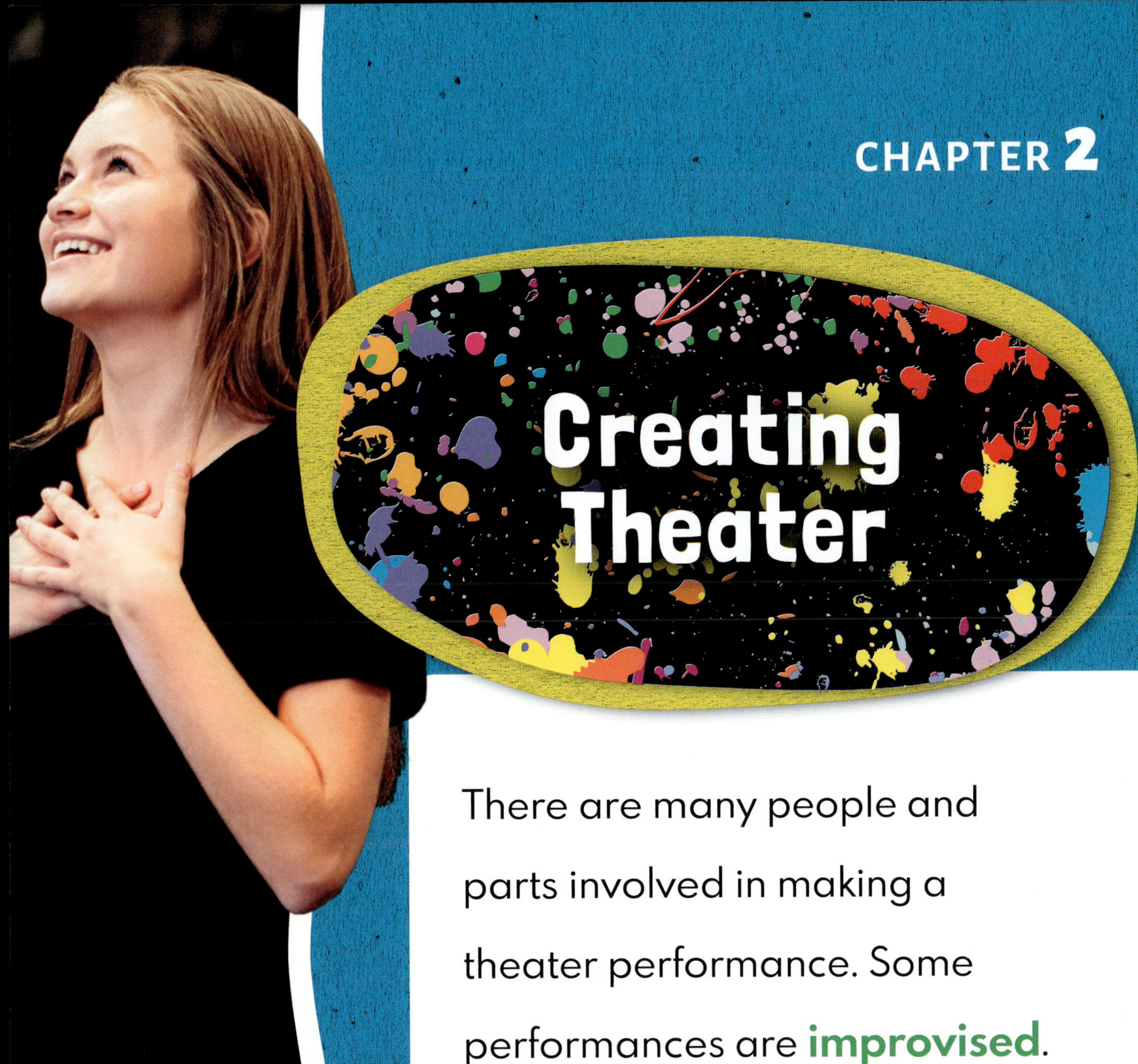

CHAPTER 2

Creating Theater

There are many people and parts involved in making a theater performance. Some performances are **improvised**. But many are scripted. A playwright writes a play's script. The script includes dialogue, or the words spoken onstage.

Types of Stages

Proscenium
The proscenium arch creates a frame over the stage.

Black box
The placement of the stage and audience change from show to show.

Thrust
The stage thrusts into the audience, with the audience seated on three sides.

In-the-round
The stage is fully surrounded by the audience on all sides.

Theaters can have different types of stages. Different stages work well for certain types of shows.

It also includes stage directions. Stage directions tell directors and actors what should happen during a scene. A composer is someone who creates the music for a show. Some composers write their own lyrics. Others work with a person called a lyricist.

Once a show is written, many people help bring it to life on stage. Directors make major decisions for a show. They also choose the performers. Musicals usually have a music director. This person helps the performers with the show's songs. Music directors also work with the people who play live music during the show. Choreographers create the dance steps.

Performers include actors, singers, and dancers. They work hard to prepare for a show.

Some performers are skilled in singing, dancing, and acting. Others may focus on only one area of performing.

First, performers must audition. If they are cast in a show, they then learn their lines or their music. They must also remember their **blocking** and choreography. When a show opens, performers act out the story for the audience.

Setting the Stage

There are many other roles that help make a show. Set designers create the setting, or scenery, onstage. Some shows take place in a

Set designers will read the script before creating a set. This helps them know what they need to build and what it will look like.

single room. For these, designers might create a highly decorated room. For other shows, designers might make sets that can move. The setting changes with the moving pieces.

Lighting designers use lights to help create the setting. Colored lights can create different moods. Spotlights help performers stand out.

Costumers decide what the performers will wear. They may sew new costumes or use existing pieces to make a costume. Hair and makeup designers style the performers.

Puppetry

Puppets can be part of theater shows. Some shows are performed with only puppets. Others use puppets alongside performers. Shadow puppets use light and shadow to create scenes. Hand puppets go on a person's hand. There are also puppets that use a performer's whole body. *The Lion King* and *Frozen* are musicals known for their puppets.

Cats is a musical famous for its makeup and costumes. The actors all play cats rather than humans.

Makeup makes it easier to see a performer's features. It can also create a character. For example, makeup designers might add wrinkles on an actor who needs to look older. Makeup can also transform a person into a creature.

Sound engineers may need to play music or sound effects during a show. They must practice playing the sounds at the right moments before the final performance.

Other important work happens behind the scenes. Sound designers create sound effects for a show. Sound engineers control the sound during a performance. They also make sure performers' microphones work correctly.

Stagehands work backstage. They do many tasks, including moving sets and raising and lowering backdrops. The stage manager is in charge of the backstage area. Stage managers give **cues** for lighting, sound, and set changes. They also make sure performers are in place before the show starts.

The audience's reactions can improve an actor's performance, which also contributes to a show. Everyone has an important role in theater.

Explore Online

Visit the website below. Does it give any new information about people in theater that wasn't in Chapter Two?

Theater

abdocorelibrary.com/art-of-theater

The New Amsterdam Theatre is one of the oldest Broadway theaters. It was built between 1902 and 1903.

CHAPTER 3

People and Places in Theater

Theater is a popular art form around the world. One of the most famous places to see a theater performance is on Broadway. Broadway is a street in New York City. But it is also a term used to describe the theater world in general.

There are 41 Broadway theaters. From 1988 to 2023, the Majestic Theatre was the home of *The Phantom of the Opera*. This was the longest-running show in Broadway history.

The West End area of London, England, is home to a major theater scene similar to Broadway. The Globe Theatre is also in London.

Tony Awards

The Tony Awards are the major theater awards ceremony in the United States. The first ceremony took place in 1947. The awards were named for Antoinette "Tony" Perry. She was an actress, director, and producer. The Tony Awards feature an awards presentation and live performances. Awards are given for acting, directing, choreography, costumes, and more.

The Globe is an open-air theater with a roof made of straw.

William Shakespeare's theater company opened the Globe in 1599. Shakespeare is one of the most famous playwrights in history. Some of his plays include *Romeo and Juliet* and *Hamlet*. The original Globe Theatre burned down, was rebuilt, and then closed. In 1997, a third Globe was built near the original's location. Today, people can see shows by Shakespeare and other playwrights there.

Lin-Manuel Miranda, *middle*, was inspired by hip-hop, rap, and pop music when writing the songs for *Hamilton*.

Theater Stars

Lin-Manuel Miranda is a famous American actor and composer. Miranda's most well-known musical is *Hamilton*. It tells the story of Alexander Hamilton, the first US secretary of the treasury. The show opened on Broadway in 2015. Miranda played Hamilton. He also wrote the **book**, music, and lyrics for the show.

Along with performing on Broadway, Audra McDonald has also starred in several movies and TV shows.

Hamilton was nominated for 16 Tony Awards and won 11, including Best Musical.

Miranda's Puerto Rican **heritage** is a major influence on his work. His first musical, *In the Heights*, tells the story of **immigrants** living in New York City. *In the Heights* also won a Tony Award for Best Musical.

Audra McDonald is an American actress. In 2014, McDonald broke a Broadway record when she won her sixth Tony Award for acting.

People can visit the Museum of Broadway to learn about famous shows, people, and costumes from throughout Broadway's history.

She has won Best Featured Actress and Best Lead Actress in both plays and musicals. She was the first actor to win in all four categories. *Ragtime* and *Porgy and Bess* are some of McDonald's most famous shows.

There is more to theater than meets the eye. From performing on stage to creating a show behind the scenes, people can get involved in theater in many ways. Participants and audiences everywhere appreciate this art form.

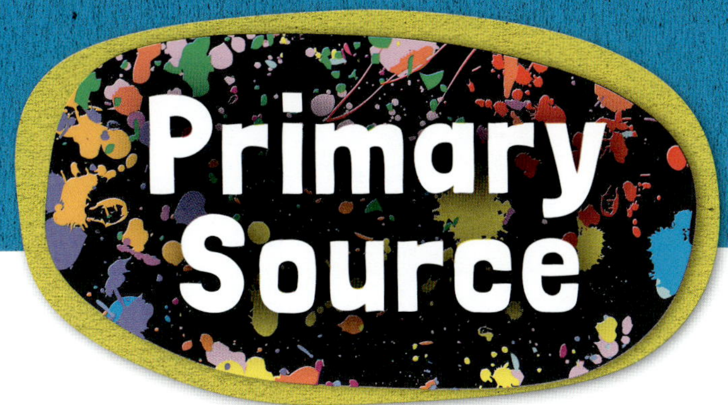

In 2024, Rick Dildine became the artistic director of the Children's Theatre Company in Minnesota. He talked about the importance of children's theater:

> For some time, I have felt that creating art for young people is the most important task artists can undertake as they expand the **scope** of American theatre.

Source: "Rick Dildine Named Artistic Director of Children's Theatre Company." *American Theatre*, 10 Jan. 2024, americantheatre.org. Accessed 22 Aug. 2024.

What's the Big Idea?

What is this quote's main idea? Explain how the main idea is supported by details.

Script

Costumes and makeup

Glossary

blocking
instructions for where to stand and what to do onstage

book
the script of a musical

chorus
a group that performs together through song or dance

cues
signals that tell actors and crew what to do in a scene

heritage
practices and characteristics that are passed down from one generation to the next

immigrants
people who move to a different country

improvised
performed without a preplanned script

scope
the range of influence that something has

Online Resources

To learn more about theater, visit our free resource websites below.

Visit **abdocorelibrary.com** or scan this QR code for free Common Core resources for teachers and students, including vetted activities, multimedia, and booklinks, for deeper subject comprehension.

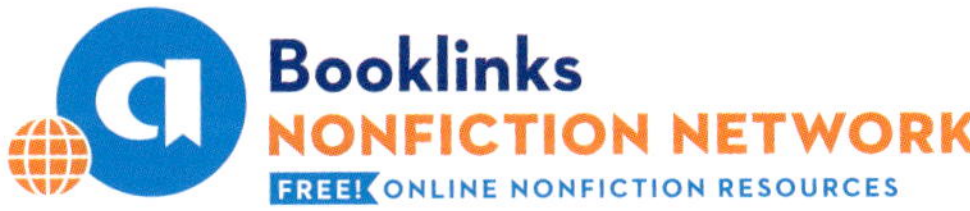

Visit **abdobooklinks.com** or scan this QR code for free additional online weblinks for further learning. These links are routinely monitored and updated to provide the most current information available.

Learn More

Matos, Elijah Rey-David. *Who Is Lin-Manuel Miranda?* Penguin Workshop, 2024.

Ransom, Candice. *The Art of Music*. Abdo, 2025.

Shaw, Mary. *The Art of Film*. Abdo, 2025.

Index

Broadway, 21–22, 24–25

choreographers, 13
costumes, 6, 16, 22

dancing, 6–8, 13–14, 22
directors, 6, 13, 22

makeup, 6, 16–17
McDonald, Audra, 25–26
Miranda, Lin-Manuel, 24–25
musicals, 5, 9, 13, 16, 24–26

performers, 13–14, 16–19
plays, 6, 8, 11, 23, 26
puppets, 16

roles, 6, 14, 19

scripts, 11
sets, 14–16, 19
Shakespeare, William, 23
singing, 6–7, 9, 13

Tony Awards, 22, 25
types of stages, 12

About the Author

K. A. Hale is a lifelong lover of theater, both as a performer and in the audience. Some of her favorite performances have been in *Sense and Sensibility*, *Mamma Mia!*, and *Grease*. She has enjoyed close to 100 shows as an audience member. Hale lives in Minnesota, where she writes, edits, and designs children's books full time.